# Breathwork

Thorsons First Directions

# Breathwork

Swami Ambikananda Saraswati

Thorsons
An Imprint of HarperCollinsPublishers
77–85 Fulham Palace Road,
Hammersmith, London W6 8JB

The Thorsons website address is:
www.thorsons.com

Published by Thorsons 2001

10 9 8 7 6 5 4 3 2 1

Text copyright © Swami Ambikananda Saraswati 2001
Copyright © HarperCollinsPublishers Ltd 2001

Text derived from Principles of Breathwork, published by
Thorsons 1999

Swami Ambikananda Saraswati asserts the moral right
to be identified as the author of this work

Editor: Nicky Vimpany
Design: Wheelhouse Creative
Production: Melanie Vandevelde
Photos from Photodisc Europe

A catalogue record for this book
is available from the British Library

ISBN 0 0071 1033 2

Printed and bound in Hong Kong

# Contents

# Breathwork

is a system that brings physical healing, emotional
through working with the breath

release and spiritual development

# Why Breathwork?

None of us needs a manual or a teacher to tell us how to take our first breath and how to carry on breathing. After emerging from the womb each of us signals our independence with a breath and a sound. That is the moment our individual life begins. From then on we live with this intimate exchange with the earth's atmosphere, breathing in and breathing out approximately 18 times a minute, 1,080 times an hour, 25,920 times each 24 hour cycle – for the rest of our lives.

In common with all other life on this planet, we humans take energy from our environment and by the power of our own alchemy transform it from one thing into another. We can survive for some days without water, for weeks without food, but only for a few moments without oxygen before major systems start to break down irrevocably. Each and every one of the 75 trillion cells in our body absorbs the oxygen we breathe in from the surrounding atmosphere and, through the process of metabolism, produces carbon dioxide which we breathe out.

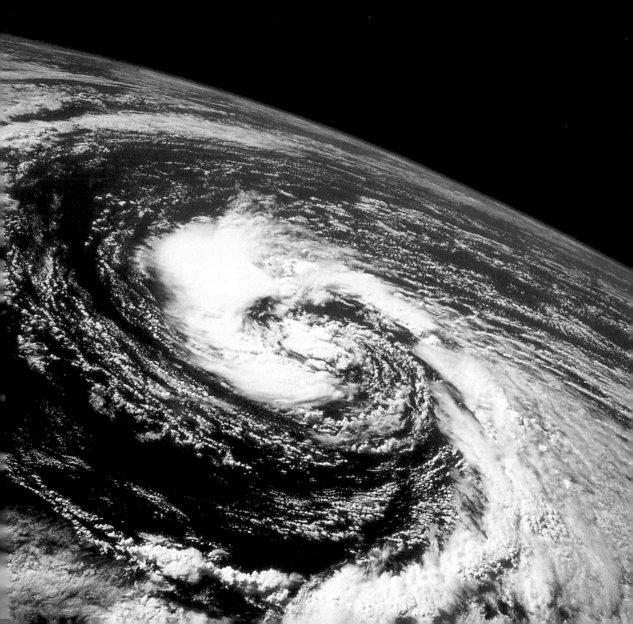

An enormous amount of research has been done this century by people dedicated to finding out how we can make better use of our bodies. Great bodywork systems, like the Alexander Technique of F. Matthias Alexander and the Reichian mind/bodywork systems that have evolved out of the work of Wilhelm Reich, have emerged from this research and are being used all over the world. All of these techniques have had to turn much of their attention to breathing. This mirrors the findings of more ancient systems like Yoga from India and Qi Gong from China, in which breathing techniques played an integral part.

As the air we breathe in becomes more and more crowded with substances other than naturally occurring gases, and as modern working practices demand that our bodies are placed in unfamiliar positions for hours on end, greater attention is being given to how we breathe and the impact our breathing habits have on our lives. Once one looks at improving how any person feels or performs, breathing soon becomes the dominant focus of attention.

When considering breathwork we span a whole spectrum of healing approaches, from the ancient to the modern, from the rational to the metaphysical, because breath is integral to all of them. It expands beyond the boundaries of healing systems into spiritual disciplines, taking seekers into what the poet Rumi called 'the breath inside the breath'.

Therein lies the true miracle of breathwork: it not only improves physical functioning but acts as a pathway inward to the self, because breath is the bridge between body and mind and between mind and spirit. To the Yogis it is the life-force and vitality of all beings. To the Romans the word for breath was spiritus, which also meant spirit, and it is the common root found in respiration, inspiration and aspiration. To the ancient Greeks breath, wind and soul were all the same.

# A Brief History of Breathwork

In the second half of the nineteenth century a French singing student in Paris, Francois Delsarte, lost his voice – apparently through poor vocal instruction. He turned to exploring his breathing and his movement. A system of movement, in which breathwork was essential, emerged from his self-study. This system was adopted and taken to America by one of his students, Steele Mackay, where it became extremely popular and where others learned and taught its methods. Most of these teachers would evolve their own method out of the original Delsarte system. In the early 1900s it returned to Europe via Germany, where a bodywork system known as Gymnastik had begun. Two of the great breathing teachers of this system were a German, Hede Kallmeyer, and an American living in Hamburg, Bess Mesendieck. Breathing teachers like Elsa Gindler emerged from the Gymnastik system and others taught by her, like the famous American teacher Carola Speads, are still teaching. Another famous breathing teacher to come from this period, who is still teaching, is the German, Ilsa Middendorf. Most recently the breathwork teacher who has created the greatest controversy is the Russian physician, Professor Konstantin Buteyko, whose method is applied specifically to people suffering from asthma. While these systems of breathwork are easily accessible in Germany, Holland, France and the USA, their popularity never reached England. In most of the United Kingdom it is in Yoga, Qi Gong and Tai Chi classes, or through systems like the Alexander Technique, that the vast majority of people will first encounter their breathing habits and begin to learn to change them. Only occasionally will a doctor refer people to be taught breathing and then it will be via a psychotherapist or physiotherapist. Physicians who are focusing on the link between habits of breathing and physical well-being, are a relatively recent phenomenon still in the minority.

**What is clear to any bodyworker, however, is that no healing system can overlook breathwork. The failure of modern medicine to do so with more focus is serious.**

# How Breathing Works

All gases follow a simple rule – they move from an area of high pressure to an area of low pressure. It is this rule that makes our bodies breathe. The air in the atmosphere exerts a certain pressure. When we have exhaled, the pressure in our thoracic cavity (the cavity in which our lungs are situated) and the pressure in the atmosphere are equal. Then powerful muscles lift and expand the ribs and cause the floor of the thoracic cavity to descend. As the cavity expands, the air in it is under less pressure than the air outside, so air flows in and we experience this as an inhalation. The body is a highly intelligent pressure gauge and as soon as enough air has entered, the muscles release – the ribs relax down and the floor of the thoracic cavity lifts. The diminishing space means the air in the cavity comes under greater pressure than the air outside, so the air flows out and we experience this as an exhalation.

# Respiration

Within the atmosphere as a whole, each individual gas produces its own pressure – this is called partial pressure. The partial pressure of any gas is dependent on the number of molecules of that gas in a mixture.

   Both oxygen and carbon dioxide travel through the lungs to and from every part of our body via the arteries and veins. At every stage we can measure the partial pressure of these gases. For instance, when air has been inhaled into the lungs, the partial pressure of oxygen in the air is greater than the partial pressure of oxygen in the blood flowing to the lungs. This is because the blood, returning from its journey through the body, is carrying mostly carbon dioxide. Following the natural law, oxygen will flow down the pressure gradient, entering the blood from the lungs until the partial pressure of oxygen is equal in the blood and the lungs. Carbon dioxide will act in exactly the same way, only going in the opposite direction.

**This whole exchange of oxygen and carbon dioxide is called respiration.**

## External and internal respiration

Inhaling and exhaling is called external respiration, and the complex and wonderful system involved in it is called the respiratory system. Muscles, primarily the diaphragm muscle, but also some powerful secondary muscles, expand the body for air to flow into the lungs, then as these muscles relax, the body contracts and the air flows out. In that space of time an exchange of gases has taken place.

Inhalation and exhalation usually take place through the nose. From the nostrils the air goes to the pharynx (back of the throat), from there to the larynx (upper throat) and trachea (throat). The trachea splits into two branches called the bronchioles. The bronchioles end in alveoli, which are minute air sacs clustered like bunches of grapes at the end of the bronchioles. It is actually in the alveoli that the exchange of gas takes place between the air in the lungs and the blood.

The process of delivering oxygen from the lungs to the rest of the body and picking up the carbon dioxide that has been produced is called internal respiration.

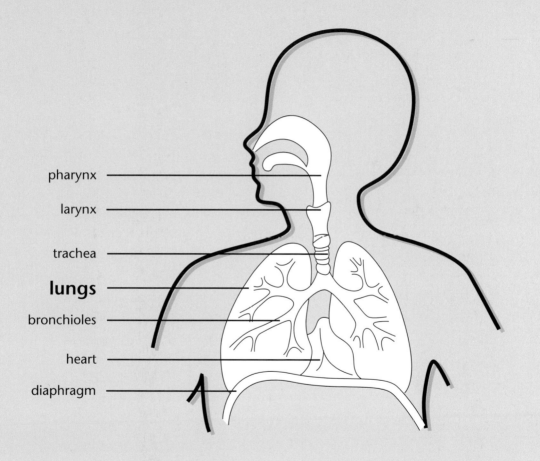

pharynx

larynx

trachea

**lungs**

bronchioles

heart

diaphragm

> **Perfect balance**
> The body will always and in all circumstances seek balance. This balance is called homeostasis. Homeostasis applies as much to breathing as it does to any other biological system.

# Metabolism

Our body uses energy on a grand scale. Most of this energy comes from burning carbohydrates in the presence of oxygen. This produces energy, carbon dioxide and water. This process of transformation is called metabolism.

Both the amount of carbohydrate and oxygen used up, and the amount of energy, carbon dioxide and water produced, depends on our energy needs at any given moment. In its constant search for homeostasis our bodies will adjust the breathing to ensure that:

- you are taking in enough oxygen for your energy requirements at the time
- the levels of carbon dioxide are maintained at an optimum level.

# pH balance

One of the most sensitive balances in our bodies is the acid/alkaline balance of our body fluids, which is called the pH balance. Breathing directly affects the body's pH balance. Because the body uses carbon dioxide to maintain its acid levels, low carbon dioxide can cause the blood to become alkaline. This can happen when someone breathes in more oxygen than they are converting to carbon dioxide, as in hyperventilation, or long-term poor breathing habits. The opposite occurs when, usually through illness, someone breathes in such a way that carbon dioxide levels rise above acceptable levels.

Low carbon dioxide levels create a condition akin to acute stress. They produce chronic fatigue, muscle cramps, chest pains, pre-menstrual syndrome, palpitations, cold feet and hands, dizziness, dry mouth, heartburn, flatulence, belching, feelings of depersonalization, impaired concentration and memory, disturbed sleep and even allergies. Remember, your body is working towards balance: if you have a habit that constantly disrupts that balance the body will try to defend itself and part of that defence is the signal it sends to change the status quo.

The list of conditions poor breathing habits can cause or aggravate is quite extensive and includes the following:

**Chronic fatigue** Your body is conditioned to respond to temporary emergencies: your mouth will go dry and your breathing become shallow and rapid. Blood will be drawn away from major organs to the extremities. This is called the flight or fight response. In the modern world, most of us are so busy that this stress has become a chronic condition and the normal 'housekeeping' functions of the body are constantly subdued.

**Chest pains** Chronic muscle cramps and spasms are a good signal of poor breathing. Loss of carbon dioxide will increase tension and spasm in muscles. This can lead to chest pains and breathlessness, which may lead people to believe they are having a heart attack.

**Pre-menstrual syndrome** In the week to ten days before the onset of menstruation a woman's progesterone levels peak, causing carbon dioxide levels in the blood to drop. If the woman is a chronic hyperventilator this drop will be in addition to the lowered level she is already living with and irritability, muscle cramps, headaches and fatigue will result.

# Contraction, expansion, equilibrium

The ancient Yogis of India saw the whole of life as being governed by three forces: expansion, contraction and equilibrium. In Sanskrit, the original language of the Yogis, these are rajas, tamas and sattva respectively. The clearest expression of these forces at work is in our breathing. We breathe in and expand, we breathe out and contract, and after the exhalation there is a brief resting phase, where we are neither breathing in nor breathing out, which corresponds to the phase of sattva, or equilibrium.

We function best, the Yogis said, when each of these phases is allowed to fulfil itself and function in harmony with the others. In fact, during the phase of equilibrium when we have breathed out, there is still air in the lungs. Between breaths an exchange of oxygen and carbon dioxide is still going on between the residual air in our lungs and our blood. This process is vital for 'levelling off' the ratio of oxygen to carbon dioxide in the blood. The body uses expansion, contraction and equilibrium to maintain balance. Poor breathing habits interfere with one of these phases and therefore with all three.

When the exquisitely sensitive balancing mechanisms of the body are able to maintain stability we experience this as a wonderful flow of energy through our entire being and a desire to live and experience life in its fullness. To achieve this we have to:

- learn to relax the abdominal and pelvic floor muscles so that the diaphragm can descend down into the belly,
- release the intercostal muscles through movement so that they can effectively pull the ribs up and away from the hips during inhalation,
- learn to intervene in the tension of muscles that are constraining the breathing process,
- become aware of the tide of air entering and leaving the body, and slow it down, and
- encourage the return of a full flow of saliva into the mouth.

Accomplishing this requires reorganizing your body's responses to your life experiences. Having taken this step backwards we can look forward at how changing the breathing affects these responses.

# Muscle Tightening

Respiration relies on the action of muscles. It is when these muscles become constricted, caught up in habitual tensions, that problems arise, because changes in breathing can have uncomfortable results. Even the smallest change can have a cascade effect that will have an enormous impact on the way we function.

## Muscles and breathing

Between breaths, during the equilibrium stage, the diaphragm muscle rests briefly. Then, at a signal from the nervous system, two bands of connective tissue, called crura, which are attached to the upper three or four lumbar vertebrae and the diaphragm muscle, make a tug. This causes the diaphragm muscle to descend, gently pushing down against the abdominal organs and intestines and making the belly go out. At the same time muscles between the ribs (the intercostal muscles) pull the ribs up and away from the hips. At another signal these muscles begin to relax and return to their resting positions, which for the diaphragm is its unique dome shape.

In a relaxed body – like that of a baby – this expansion and contraction is easily visible to any observer. We can see that full and complete breathing is not dependent on the lungs but on muscles. However, the truth is that if something goes wrong with one muscle this will have a wave effect through the whole musculature of the body. As Michael Grant White, a breathwork teacher puts it:

*Your shoulder muscles can restrict your breathing. Your chest muscles can restrict your breathing. Your ankle muscles can restrict your breathing.*

Many other muscles need to work in concert with the diaphragm and intercostals to achieve full respiration. Sustained contraction or chronic tension of any of these will compromise breathing in general. Muscles can become restricted for a number of reasons including poor posture and accidents like falling or bumping into things. However, most of our muscle restrictions are the result of an habitual action we have set up in our bodies in response to the lives we live.

Wilhelm Reich, whose work led to the advent of several body-based psychotherapies, was the first person to speak of 'muscle armouring'. Blocked breathing, to Reich, was essentially caused by this muscle armouring. He maintained that, in response to the environment, the free and uninhibited breathing of a baby is gradually eroded. The baby, exquisitely sensitive to its world, sensing internal needs that it has to suppress because of the responses their expression evokes in the carers around it, begins to tighten muscles – primarily the diaphragm muscle. This tightening will then continue to the pelvis, chest, back, legs and throat. The muscle never returns spontaneously to its original resting state but remains rigid and drawn in throughout childhood and into adulthood. Thus the process of expansion, contraction and equilibrium is compromised. Sometimes it is not so compromised as to cause problems that demand our attention – there will just be the occasional nagging headache and background fatigue. Sometimes it is compromised enough to cause extreme symptoms.

**To overcome muscle armouring and inward contraction, the very first thing that has to be addressed is the chronic holding patterns of the abdominal and pelvic floor muscles. There are several bodywork therapies that address this problem.**

All Reichian methods – including **Bioenergetics,** developed by Alexander Lowen – focus on releasing body tension and returning one to full and creative breathing. Alexander Lowen was a student of Reich, and his bodywork system, Bioenergetics, is based on the work of Reich. In the words of Lowen, 'Bioenergetics is a therapeutic technique to help a person get back together with his body and to help him enjoy to the fullest degree possible the life of the body.' It is essential that a therapist is present, as the return to deep abdominal breathing requires the release of blocked emotions through the expression of these emotions. The therapist places the person in postures that will bring to the surface whatever emotion caused the muscles to become inhibited initially, and then encourages the full release of that emotion in the therapy session.

**The Alexander Technique** – named after the Australian actor who developed it – takes a different approach. After Alexander had suffered from a loss of voice, he spent a number of years critically watching how his use of his own body stood in the way of his full use of voice. In order to breathe and move more freely, with more poise and grace, Alexander said change was necessary – and that 'Change involves carrying out an activity against the habit of a lifetime.' The Alexander Technique insists it is not a therapy but a technique that can be taught. A teacher will take a student through a number of everyday tasks: sitting, standing, walking, lying down and, of course, breathing, guiding him or her in learning how to intervene in habits to arrive at a better use of themselves. Through practising everyday tasks these new habits become embedded and can then be carried over into more complex tasks and situations.

Like the Alexander Technique, **Yoga** requires the presence of a teacher. The teacher gives guidance, but it is essential that the process is carried out on your own and on a regular basis. This is partly because the process immediately involves conscious breathing as a means of release, not only as a result. Yoga does not require the full recall of any of the emotions that may have provoked a life-long habit of tension. To the Yogi, the tightened, tense muscle is the body's way of remembering the trauma, and restoring that muscle to its resting length is the complete release.

# Sensing Resistance

To begin your journey towards the freedom of fuller breathing you can adopt the following techniques. They are simple, effective and safe. They are adapted from techniques taught to me by a great Indian teacher, and include some of the directional instructions of the Alexander Technique as an aid.

It is quite common for therapists to ask people to lie down on their back to begin to focus on their breathing. My own experience has been that this is not particularly useful. When we lie down the space of the thorax is reduced because the abdominal cavity spreads upward. The picture we therefore get of the breathing is one that is true only for while we are lying down and awake. Furthermore, for most people, their lower back and pelvis areas are too stiff for this to be a comfortable posture and the tension in these areas actually increases while lying in this posture.

Adopting a Yoga posture called Pose of the Moon (see diagram below) one can focus on how the body is moving with the breath.

## Pose of the moon

If you are unable to sit back onto your calves and heels, place a firm cushion or folded blanket under your buttocks; and if your head is unable to comfortably reach the floor, place a thickish, soft-covered book under your forehead. However, if you really are quite unable to get into this pose, then use its variation – sitting on a chair.

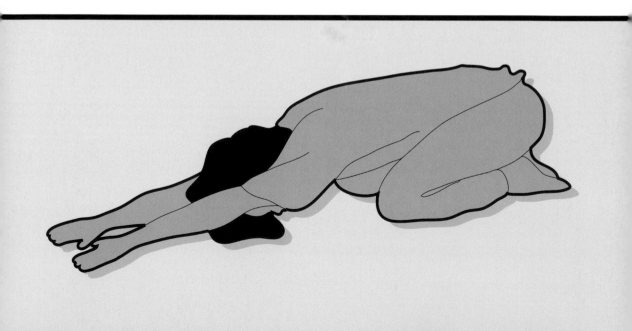

## Forward sitting pose

In the Forward Sitting Pose (see diagram overleaf) ensure that the seat of the chair is high enough to have your thighs parallel to the floor and that you have your feet flat on the floor. Then pivot forward from the hips, lean your elbows on your thighs, bend your arms at the elbows and place your hands on the opposite thighs. Be careful not to let your shoulders come up around your ears and keep your back, neck and head flowing in a straight line. Now begin to give your body direction: be careful – you are not doing anything, you are simply communicating.

- Think of your weight releasing down.
- Feel your sitting bones meeting the chair and feel the support of the floor beneath your feet.
- Allow your body weight to flow down into the floor through the sitting bones and the structure of the chair and through your legs into your feet.
- Let go – release your hold on your spine and allow it to flow up, releasing any tension in the back of your neck, allowing the muscles in the back of the neck to lengthen.
- Only after you feel comfortable in this posture do you drop your head forward – not pushing it, simply letting its own weight take it gently down without letting the shoulders pull up.

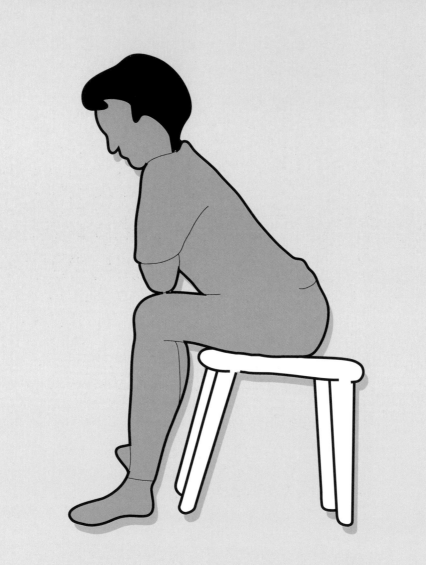

In either of these postures you are ready to begin to focus on your breathing:

**Exercise: watching your breath**

Become aware of any movement you sense in your abdomen. Try not to be concerned if you feel nothing – you are not making judgements, you are becoming aware. Keep in mind all the time that you are a living being able to change.

Then move your attention to your back, particularly the lower back. Do you sense any movement there? Can you feel any muscles in the lower back expanding and releasing with the inhalation and the exhalation? Are you aware of any movement in the spine at all?

Is there any moment of pause between the exhalation and the next inhalation?

Finally, begin to count your inhalation and exhalation. Are they the same length? Is one longer than the other? Make a note of all the results of your observations.

I recommend that you remain in this posture for no longer than five minutes at a time, watching your breathing, then release and do something else. Come back to it later. Little and often is best in the beginning.

Here are a couple of questions students ask me at this stage which you may find helpful:

**Question**: After just a few seconds of watching my breath my mind wanders off and I lose focus. It's very frustrating. Is there anything I can do?

**Answer**: The nature of the mind is to wander. The most important thing is not to try too hard. If your mind wanders off, gently bring it back to focusing on breathing. Gradually, over months and years, the mind will become retrained.

**Question**: Very soon after focusing on my breathing I start getting real feelings of panic. These often make me break off and do something else. What can I do?

**Answer**: You are fortunate – it usually takes people months to become aware that they are in a chronic state of panic! When you feel panic, you move away from the pain. I am asking you not to give in to that impulse to immediately move away – to stay with the pain long enough to find the right direction to move in. Moving away from the pain means it will always be mysterious, an unknown quantity that has the power to strike at any time. The pain will point us in the right direction. So, stay with the panic, breathe into it, try and breathe right through it, exhale it. In this way you are allowing the panic to communicate its message to you.

# Breath and the Mind

Isaac Newton left us with the legacy of a relentlessly mechanistic world view: a separation of mind and body that persists to this day. Even though modern physics has overturned many of Newton's theories, it is still hard for us to accept that the body and the mind are one organism rather than two separate units. In the field of breathing, a great deal of research supports the non-dual position. Studies suggest that not processing a traumatic event creates a 'significant' physical stress. The trauma is expressed in and communicated by the body through tense muscles and inappropriate breathing habits.

Outside stressors are constant for all of us, but our way of dealing with them can change – and breath is one of the most powerful means of both investigating the trauma and making the change. Before we look at a common breathing disorder and how it may be a manifestation of body/mind oneness, try an awareness exercise to see if you can experience this oneness through your breath.

## Body-mind awareness exercise

- Adopt the Forward Sitting Pose (*see pages* 27–28), following the directions until your mind is able to focus on your breathing.

- Become aware of how much your abdomen and/or chest expands with each breath, as well as the frequency of inhalations and exhalations. Try not to count them – simply allow your mind to become familiar with them.

- Now, for just a few seconds think of something that frightens you – either something from your past or a fear you have now. Conjure up as vivid an image as possible, then switch your attention back to your breathing. (As I am unable to swim, I am frightened of entering large bodies of water. So, whenever I have to do this exercise I think of being in the sea or in a large lake.)

    Did you notice any change at all? Did simply holding an image of something frightening change the rate or depth (or both) of your breathing? Try the same exercise again, thinking of something pleasant this time, and make a note of your responses.

# Asthma

Asthma is a common breathing disorder. Indeed, about five per cent of the population has asthma and that figure is on the increase. No-one actually knows what the cause of asthma is, despite enormous research. Initially it was thought to be a bronchial spasm that could be triggered by any one of a number of factors, including pollen, pollution and house dust. Deeper probing has revealed that inflammation of the airways is present before the trigger is present and that this inflammation is an immune response. The theory examined opposite, put forward by Dr Buteyko, that this immune response is the body defending itself in the face of falling carbon dioxide levels, has not yet been widely accepted by the medical establishment.

# The Buteyko method

One of the most controversial treatments for asthma is the Buteyko method. A trial of the method done in Brisbane, Australia, showed an astonishing 90 per cent decrease in the use of relief drugs needed to deal with the symptoms. Buteyko's method involves the sufferer in changing their breathing habits rather than relying on medication to overcome their symptoms. This is because Buteyko claims it is the way we breathe that is causing the inflammation, restriction and mucus build-up in the air passages.

According to Buteyko, asthma is caused by hyperventilation that has upset the delicate balance between oxygen and carbon dioxide to the extent that the delivery of oxygen to the cells is slowed down. The brain and internal organs are deprived of the oxygen they need, which causes the body to breathe more, which lowers further the level of carbon dioxide. The body then tries to protect itself from these falling levels of carbon dioxide by restricting the air passages.

The solution for Buteyko is to have the asthma patient slow down their breathing and allow for the natural pause in breathing between exhalation and inhalation, thus giving the body an opportunity to normalize its carbon dioxide level. His method then goes one step further to retrain the brain to adjust to the new carbon dioxide levels.

The Buteyko method seems to be having excellent results in reducing the symptoms of asthma for many sufferers. Add to this other bodywork techniques like Yoga, the Alexander Technique, Bioenergetics or any other of the numerous mind-body techniques now available for addressing the body's organization around its history, and you begin to effect a release of the tension that the body-mind organism is holding. This creates a more fundamental healing process because you are addressing the habits of tension in the whole organism.

Chronic, hidden tension is a body-mind phenomenon and it appears that there is a whole organism response that in one person may be asthma, in another fatigue, and in another muscle cramps or panic attacks. The entire organism acts as one – both to adjust to the change and to communicate its distress.

**Conscious breathing offers the most direct route to the unconscious tensions that we all hold. It also offers a means of release from those tensions that involves the entire body-mind organism, inviting it to experience its wholeness.**

# Breathing Towards Clarity

What we can see is that our breathing is not separate from our collective human history, our individual past or our environment. What we can do is begin to intervene in our chronic stress-holding patterns in order to liberate our breathing – because breathing is not a matter of the lungs moving, but the whole body moving: contracting and expanding and resting in equilibrium.

In this chapter we will look at different segments of the body, how we hold tension in these areas and how we can gently begin to release them. Then we will look at experiencing full body breathing.

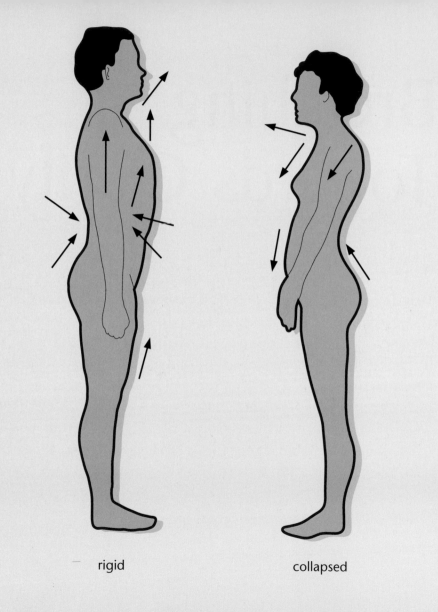

rigid                    collapsed

To begin with, however, let us look at two body types that are extremes that inhibit full body breathing. These are the 'rigid' and 'collapsed' bodies described by Stanley Keleman, in his book *Emotional Anatomy*. The rigid body, Keleman says, is the body braced against disapproval and insult. The collapsed body is the body that has caved in under the weight of such disapproval and insult.

### Exercise

Begin by getting an idea of your own posture. Next time you are naked, take a few moments to look at yourself in a full-length mirror. Examine both the full frontal and side views. You will probably find that you are not at either of these extremes of rigid or collapsed, but somewhere in the middle, with elements of each. Your shoulders may be raised and/or rotated slightly forward; or your neck may incline forward and your chin jut out; your lumbar spine might sweep inward and your lower back lift up  Try not to become involved in making judgements, simply observe. Observe your shoulders for a moment, see if they lift and descend – or move at all – with your breathing.

Once you have a visual image of your holding patterns it is time to go for a deeper experience: looking inward at yourself. Turning our senses in on ourselves is our very first step towards self-knowledge. It is also the most powerful means available for bringing about change.

# The whole in parts

The body segments as I present them here are loosely based on the observations of Wilhelm Reich, modified by my own experience. The methods of release are derived from a combination of Yoga and the Alexander Technique. The segments are: the eyes, forehead, nose, temples and scalp; the jaw, ears and base of the skull; the throat and the back of the neck; the heart and lungs; the navel area; the pelvic area; the legs and feet.

Tension in any of these areas will inhibit breathing. Releasing tension from any of these areas will liberate breathing. From now on it is better to sense rather than trying to get feedback from a mirror. If you don't have time to go through all the segments in one session, complete the first three, then break and return to the other four later, running a quick check through the first three before you begin. The most important thing to remember is that the more you learn to sense your inner self the easier it becomes.

# The eyes, forehead, nose, temples and scalp

### Exercise

Begin investigating and releasing these segments seated on a dining room chair, with a pillow in the small of your back. Check through the following:

- If you were to locate the 'I' of 'I am' would you locate it in this head/brain centre? Many people forget that the 'I' is a whole body 'I'. Ask yourself, 'Where do I locate "I"?'
- Do the outer corners of your eyes feel pinned back towards the temples and do the lower lids feel as if they are working, holding up the eye, focusing?
- Now check your breathing. What is its rate, where are you breathing, where are you experiencing movement?
- Go back to the eyes and feel their relationship with the forehead and the relationship of the forehead with the scalp. Where you sense tightness can you consciously let it go as you let the breath go during an exhalation?
- If you wear spectacles all the time it is important to leave them on and sense whether this segment experiences any tension in 'holding' them.

Now you are ready to do a simple exercise with the eyes. Do this very slowly and with great attention. There should be no effort here, you are looking 'through' the floor with a restful gaze.

### Excercise

- Let your eyes rest on the floor about six feet in front of you. Try not to look at the floor but through it. This is called Tratak, The Restful Gaze. Now gradually become aware of your whole field of vision. Resist the urge for your eyes to dart around and simply remain gazing at the floor in front of you.
- Gently turn your head round to the right. Do not let your eyes dart forward or backward. Allow your gaze to flow with the movement of your head. Repeat to the left, then bring your gaze back to the centre.
- Check in with your breathing: has it changed as you are doing this?

Try and repeat parts of this exercise through the day. Stop wherever you are and let your gaze just rest some distance away.

Maintaining the restful gaze, turn your awareness to your nose:

### Exercise
- Feel the cool air entering through both nostrils as you breathe in, feel it hitting the back of your throat before it descends and warms. Then feel the warm air that rises up from the throat leaving through both your nostrils.
- Do both nostrils carry the same amount of air, or is one feeling slightly closed? Which one? This is a perfectly normal phenomenon. One nostril is always slightly more dilated than the other and this switches throughout the day.
- If you are unsure, just lightly clip shut one nostril and feel the flow of breath in the other, then repeat on the other side. Another effective way of measuring is just to breathe out onto a small hand-held mirror and you will see there is a greater area of vapour left on the mirror on one side – the side that is more open at the time of the test.

One of the commonest reasons for breathing disorders and mouth breathing is one or both nostrils being constantly blocked. There could be a number of reasons for this: a cold; an allergy response; nasal polyps or a deviated septum.

**Nasal polyps**: A persistent swelling in the lining of the nose due to lingering sinus congestion. If you suspect this it is advisable to visit a good herbalist to see if they can help clear the infection and establish its source, or see an ear, nose and throat specialist.

**Deviated septum**: The septum is the wall between the nostrils and it normally runs in a straight line from the nostrils to the base of the skull. However, it is not uncommon for the septum to deviate from this straight line and obstruct the breathing.

In winter, when many people in the Northern hemisphere use central heating, the atmosphere in homes can become far too dry. If your nose begins to feel dry and tender, introduce a humidifier to add some moisture to the atmosphere.

## The jaw, ears and base of the skull

This can be an area of chronic tension. The powerful jaw muscles may have become accustomed to clenching the teeth, and the tongue may have become accustomed to a remarkable rigidity. This is not surprising when you consider the number of times people suppress what they want to say.

## Exercise

- Remaining seated on the chair, take your attention to the base of your skull. You will probably find this area feels as if it is being pulled down by the back of the neck, giving your chin an upward tilt and pulling down on the back of your head. Once you have become aware of these sensations, check in with your breathing, feeling its rhythm and rate.

- Now, allow the base of the skull to become 'unhinged' and float upwards. As you do, the chin might drop slightly and your forehead tilt forward. Check in with your breathing again.

- Next we come to the jaw. Are your teeth meeting? Even if they are meeting just lightly it indicates the presence of tension in the jaw muscles.

- Check your tongue – is it pressing against the roof of your mouth or is it lying relaxed and making more contact with the floor of the mouth?

- To release the jaw, try a variation of a Yoga posture called The Lion's Breath. Breathe in through your nose, and as you breathe out open your mouth wide and throw your tongue out as far as you can. If you do it a few times you should begin to make a sound with it – like the roar of a lion coming from deep within you.

- If the Lion's Breath feels too extreme, try this instead. Open out your right hand and rest your chin on the inner edge between thumb and fingers.
- Exert a downward pressure with your hand, letting your jaw loosen and pulling it down. Synchronize this movement with your breath, breathing out as you pull the jaw down.
- Once you have repeated this exercise a few times check the base of the skull has not latched itself to that downward pull again – if it has let it release. Check in with your breathing and take your attention to your cheeks and ears.
- Become aware of how 'set' the muscles of the cheeks may be. Often these muscles hold an anticipatory tension for speech or smiling. Simply become aware of the tension and feel it melting away.
- Become aware of your ears. Now employ your powerful imagination and imagine that you are breathing through the ears. Feel that each inhalation and exhalation is happening through the ears and that you are breathing a sense of peace into the ears and allowing it to fill the skull and mouth and flow down through the throat.

## The throat and back of the neck

The throat and neck represent the slender link between the head and the heart. Again, this is a depository of much tension. Begin by just becoming aware of the whole throat and neck and how the head balances on top of the neck. Then gently proceed with checking and releasing this area:

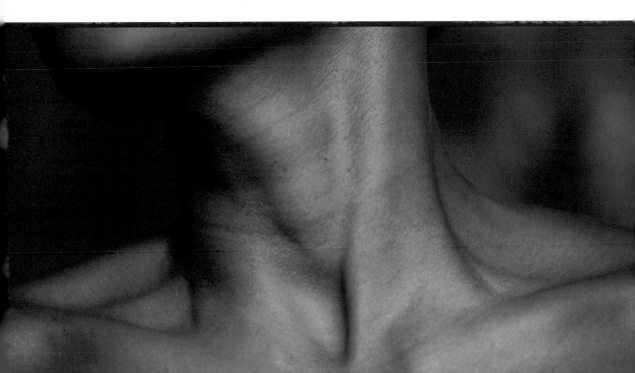

### Exercise

- Become aware of any feelings of constriction in the throat. Remaining aware of this, breathe in through the nose, feeling the cool air flowing down your throat. As you breathe out, allow your jaw to drop and release the breath with a long whispered 'Ahhh..' Feel the tension in the throat leaving with the out-breath. With each 'ahhh' feel your throat opening more and more.

- Become aware of the back of the neck. The back of the neck and the lumbar region of the spine are the most mobile areas of the back and problems in one usually reflect problems in the other. Begin by feeling your sitting bones and feet contacting the support beneath them. Breathe in, and as you breathe out release your weight down through your sitting bones into the chair and down through your legs into the floor. Repeat this focus for two or three breaths and allow the muscles of the neck to release and lengthen.

- Breathe in and, as you breathe out, allow your head to drop forward. Be careful not to push it down – let its own weight carry it down. Keep releasing it for a full inhalation and exhalation and then slowly raise your head and allow it to balance on top of the neck.

- Next, breathe in and, as you breathe out, allow your head to release to the right, dropping your right ear towards your right shoulder. You will feel a gentle stretch up the left side of the neck. Allow your shoulders to release. Hold this for a full inhalation and exhalation and slowly raise the head. Repeat to the other side.

- To help release the muscles of the neck, turn your head as if you are going to look over your right shoulder but stop halfway so that your nose is pointing mid-way between the front and the right shoulder. Take a full breath in and as you breathe out allow your head to drop towards the back over your right shoulder. Hold this for a full inhalation and exhalation and then gently raise your head. Repeat to the left.

## The heart and lungs

This is the area that most people associate with breathing: when we want to take a deep breath the tendency is to heave and expand the upper chest. However, breathing requires the co-operation of the entire body. More than any other, this is an area we protect vigorously. We tense our shoulders and allow this tension to carry down to our arms and hands. We rotate the shoulders forward and tighten up. We even call the wonderful, mobile bones that surround and protect the heart and lungs, the rib cage. What is it that we feel will escape or invade? While you are keeping blows out you are also keeping emotions in. And emotions are not meant to be kept in – they are meant to flow. When they do flow freely, everything softens, the ribs become less like a cage and more like wings, lifting up and away from the sturdy hips that keep us grounded.

**Exercise**

- Become aware of any holding pattern in your shoulders. Visualize your shoulders widening and consciously allow them to let their weight go.
- Place a hand over your breastbone and feel for any movement.
- Place your hands over your ribs on either side and feel their powerful movement as you breathe.
- Rest your hands on your back and see if you can detect any movement in your thoracic spine as you breathe – can you feel your back widening at all as you breathe in, and contracting as you breathe out?

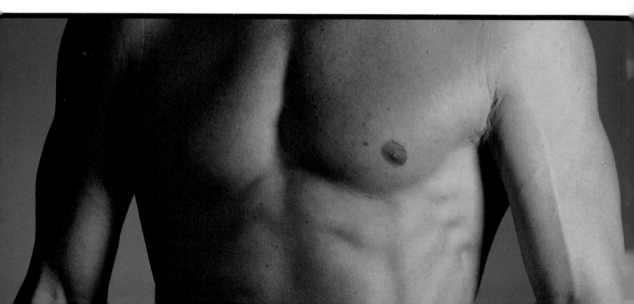

Here are a few release exercises for this area:

**Exercise**

- Take your hands back, opening your chest, and take hold of the chair legs, just below the seat, so that the backs of the hands are facing out.
- Breathe in, lifting your breastbone, pushing the thoracic vertebrae forward. As you breathe out, release. Repeat this three or four times. This exercise stretches the powerful muscles in front of the shoulders and mobilizes the breastbone.
- Breathe in, bringing your left arm up over your head, and as you breathe out, drop your hand back as if you are holding a tray in the air. At the same time release your shoulder. Then breathe in, stretching the heel of your hand upwards towards the ceiling. Feel the stretch through the left side of your body. Breathe out, releasing the stretch but keeping the arm overhead. Repeat this for three breaths and on the last exhalation slowly lower your arms. Repeat this exercise with your right arm.

## The navel area

The navel area really consists of the entire abdomen – the belly. It has been my experience that professionals from Western orthodox medicine will focus on this area in particular when attempting to correct breathing habits. Good breathing to them is abdominal breathing.

Releasing tension from the belly is indeed of vital importance to full and complete breath because only this will allow the diaphragm muscle to descend to its fullest extent. But it is the experience of Yoga teachers, Alexander teachers and a number of other bodywork therapists that focusing on this area simply serves to increase the tension in the area. It has also been our observation that people are quite capable of breathing poorly – often in a hyperventilating pattern – by using the abdomen. What also has to be remembered is that this area includes the lumbar area of the back where there is often incredible tension.

The following awareness techniques and exercises are taken from Yoga:

**Exercise 1**
- Remain seated and place both hands over your navel. Notice whether the belly moves in or out as you breathe in and whether it moves back as you breathe out. The correct movement is for the abdomen to move out on inhalation.
- Drop forward into Forward Sitting Pose (*see page* 28). Become aware of the lumbar area of your back. As you breathe, focus on this area and see if you can feel the muscles here expanding out to the side as you breathe in and coming back as you breathe out. When you have connected with this movement sit back up.
- Now place one hand over your navel again and move the other hand to the same position on your back. Feel the movement under your hands and whether there is expansion as you breathe in and contraction as you breathe out.

Now that you have got to know the movement in this area you can try some ancient Yoga techniques for correcting and releasing breathing. For the following exercise you will have to stand up:

## Exercise 2

- Place your feet about three feet apart with your toes facing 'ten to two', and bend your knees slightly.

- Lean forward and rest your hands on your thighs just above your knees. Do not allow your shoulders to pull up around your ears. Release your weight down through your legs, into the floor, and allow your lower back to release and descend.

- Breathe in normally. Take your focus to the out-breath. As you breathe out, pull your belly inwards and slightly upwards in a powerful contraction. At the same time, drop your tailbone further and 'tuck' it under as you arch the lumbar area of your back. Hold the breath out in this way for just a second and then relax your abdomen and breathe in normally. Repeat this three or four times and then take a break.

- Sit back in the chair and place your hands over your abdomen again noticing any changes that have occurred in the movement of your belly.

## The pelvic area

This is an area of considerable tension for most people – brought about by anything from potty training to sexual anxieties. In Yoga this area is referred to as *kanda*, a Sanskrit word meaning 'root'. Housing our reproductive organs, sexual organs and organs of elimination, tension here can cause wide-ranging problems. The muscles of this area need to be soft, relaxed and welcoming to the descending diaphragm.

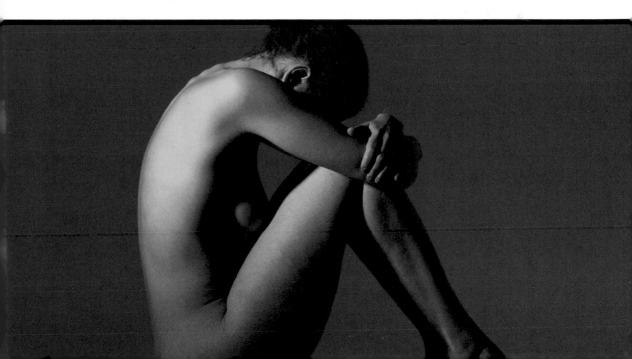

**Exercise 3**

- Sit in the chair and place your hands over your lower belly. Feel its movement as you breathe. Is there any movement at all? Is it also expanding out with the abdomen or does it remain still?
- Now check your lower back and sitting bones. Is your back releasing down with the weight falling through the sitting bones, or are you sitting and pulling up your tailbone, creating tension in the lumbar spine?

To begin to release the muscles in this area try the following exercises:

**Exercise 4**

- Lie down on your back on a mat on the floor. Bend your knees and hug both legs into your chest. As you do this feel the whole of your spine coming into contact with the floor and allow your weight to release through the spine and into the earth.
- Release your left leg and slowly straighten it, resting it on the floor.
- Release your right leg and hug the left leg into your chest.
- Repeat, alternating between the left and right leg, holding each leg for about three or four breaths.
- Sit up and bring the soles of your feet together with your knees pointing outward, wrap your hands around your feet. Allow your knees to become heavy and relax down.

- Take a deep breath in and raise your knees just a couple of inches. As you breathe out, whisper 'Ahhhh', letting your knees release down. Be careful not to pull your lower back up – let all your weight fall down through your sitting bones.

There is a powerful muscle, called the iliopsoas muscle, that connects the lumbar vertebrae, the front of the hip and the femur (the upper leg bone). I have noticed time and again that if this muscle is in even a slight contraction it can be felt at the shoulders. What I advise, because this is such a powerful muscle, is that you do a simple exercise to release and gently stretch it:

## Exercise 5

- Come up onto your knees and bring your left leg forward, placing the foot on the floor. Push the left foot forward so that there is an angle of about 45 degrees between the thigh and the lower leg. Rest your hands on your thigh.
- Breathe in and as you breathe out let your weight slowly sink down so that you feel the gentle stretch up the front of your right thigh. Be careful not to let your body tip forward – if you do that you will lose the stretch.
- Repeat this with the right leg brought forward.

## The legs and feet

Ill-fitting but fashionable shoes often leave our feet distorted and unhappy. One of the first things we do to relax is kick off our shoes. The bare foot is able to splay itself on the ground, making proper contact through which the body can release its weight and renew its vital connection to the earth. The buildings we have created and the shoes we constrain our feet in are gradually making us lose our connection with the earth. Another tendency of both the rigid body and the collapsed body is to lock the knees back in what is called hyperextension. Contrary to popular belief, this is not a straight leg, it is a posture in which the whole body weight falls onto the lower back. In order to allow the weight to fall down through the legs and into the earth, the skin at the back of the knees should be soft. Then it is possible to release the tailbone, soften the buttocks and let the weight fall, going through the feet into the earth.

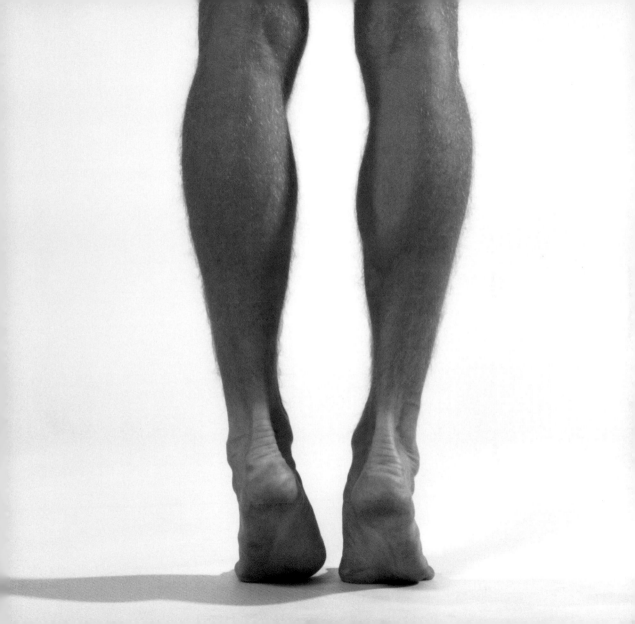

# Whole body breathing

There is an invigorating sequence of Yoga postures called Salute to the Sun. This part of it is an excellent way of renewing the contact and communication between all the segments of the body and it is best done before whole body breathing awareness:

- Go onto all fours again on a rug or mat, with your knees slightly apart under the hips and your hands under your shoulders with the fingers slightly splayed. Tuck in your toes.
- Breathe in and, as you breathe out, drop your chest and chin onto the floor, pushing your buttocks up.
- Breathe in and as you breathe out straighten your legs, relaxing your feet and releasing your pelvis and chin so that your whole body is flat on the floor.
- Relax your buttocks and let your pelvis and thighs sink into the floor.
- Breathe in and push up with your arms, bringing your head, shoulders and chest off the floor.
- Breathe out and come back up onto all fours and sit back onto your heel, body forward and arms stretched out in Pose of the Moon. Repeat this three times and on the last time bring your arms to your side, sliding your hands behind you.

To be aware of your whole body breathing remain in the Pose of the Moon (*see page* 26), placing a folded blanket or towel under your buttocks and a soft covered book under your forehead if that is more comfortable. Then do the following awareness sequence:

- Become aware of your abdomen pushing into your thighs as you breathe in and releasing as you breathe out.
- Become aware of your lower back, the sacrum and the lumbar vertebrae lifting like driftwood on a wave as you breathe in and releasing as you breathe out.
- Become aware of your whole back widening as you breathe in and contracting as you breathe out.
- Become aware of your anus and genitalia gently expanding and opening as you breathe in and contracting lightly as you breathe out.
- Become aware of your whole envelope of skin expanding as you breathe in and contracting as you breathe out.

Try and do this sequence two or three times a week in the beginning as you are trying to change your breathing.

# The Soul of Breathing

At the heart of the spiritual teachings of the most ancient cultures of the earth we find breathwork. All these teachings hold that a knowledge of self must be gained for enlightenment to happen, and that the only means of gaining self-knowledge is by turning the vision inwards. The path that vision must then follow is the path of the breath. This is most beautifully stated by the Vietnamese Buddhist monk, the Reverend Thich Nhat Hanh:

*Breathing and knowing that we are breathing is a basic practice. No one can be truly successful in the art of meditating without going through the door of breathing.*

# The essential vitality

**To the Yogis breath is much more than the inhalation of oxygen and the exhalation of carbon dioxide. To the Yogi breath is prana – the essential vitality that all life is dependent upon.**

This prana precedes creation and all creation issues from it. Prana is the life-force of all things: the exuberance and vitality behind all life and permeating all life. Consciousness of the movement of prana is gained through conscious breathing.

Behind material form and function, the Yogis say, a vibrant pranic body operates and by its operation the material world comes into being, renews itself and eventually dissolves back into the elements. The human body, along with all of manifest creation, emerges from that all-pervasive pranic vibration. To the Yogis prana is organized, through the breath, under the primacy of the panchatattva – the five thatnesses.

# The five thatnesses

The Yogis saw that the properties of the earth are reflected in us and we therefore have a quality, a thatness, of the earth. The word tattva literally means thatness, and they named and described five (pancha) of them: prithvi (**earth**), apas (**water**), agni (**fire**), vayu (**air**), akasha (**space**). Prana, they said, is organized by these tattva within us, and each tattva has a specific place of focus.

## Prithvi – the Earth

Prithvi, the earth focus, is situated at the perineum. Breath reaching there is transformed into the vitality that gives **stability, support and cohesion.** Through the power of prithvi we feel grounded, secure, with a sense of belonging. It governs our sense of smell. If this prana is disturbed we lose our balance and become confused about our purpose. Physically we lose bone mass. Those in whom this focus is strong are well-built, giving, non-judgemental, supportive people. If this becomes unbalanced they can easily become stuck and rigid.

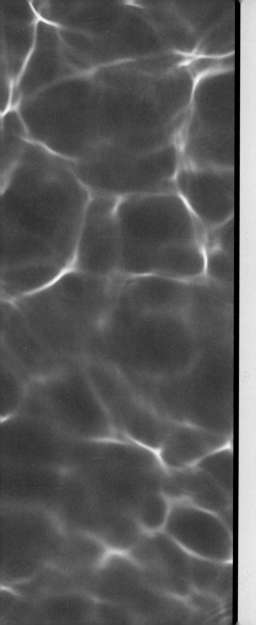

## Apas – Water

Apas, which means to pervade, has its focus at the base of the spine. It transforms breath into the vitality that imparts the **ability to create**. It gives us our sexual potency and reproductive capacities. The artist, the writer, the gardener and the scientist are all using creative abilities provided by apas tattva. When this tattva is disturbed we lose the capacity to access the creative power of water. This water is also said to be our ancient memory – the genetic pattern that carries within it the entire history of creation. People in whom this focus is strongest are usually **deep thinkers and philosophers**. When it becomes unbalanced however, they can become morose, depressed and uncommunicative.

## Agni – Fire

Agni is our capacity for **transformation** – we breathe in oxygen and transform it through our own alchemy into something else. More than any other tattva Agni gives us our **personal ambience** – the quality that people can feel and are aware of long before we speak to each other. It is also the ability to transform ideas and information into that which we can use. People in whom this tattva is strong will be the 'rainmakers' in our society. These are the people who change the whole atmosphere in a room by just walking in and who can sell you ice in winter. Situated behind the navel, Agni governs our **sense of sight and our vision of ourselves**. Unbalanced it can mean highs and lows – as in manic depression.

## Vayu – Air

Vayu also means wind. Situated behind the heart, this focus gives prana its **capacity for movement**. This movement of prana, transformed by the tattvas, throughout our body is under the governorship of vayu. We can see each tattva expressed in each cell: each cell has cohesion (prithvi), has the capacity to recreate itself (apas), to transform nutrients into energy (agni), to move (vayu), and to organize itself (akasha). Vayu is also our capacity of movement in the world we are born into – the **grace and fluidity** with which we move through that world. It is also the **movement of thought** – the quickness of our ideas. It governs our sense of touch and our ability to be touched. Those in whom this focus is strongest will display great leadership qualities. When this tattva becomes unbalanced we may become impulsive and reckless.

## Akasha – Space

The last of the five tattvas, situated at the base of the throat, is akasha – space. This is the beginning of creation, the ability to make **order out of chaos**. This is prana converted into the capacity to sustain and organize the instructions held in the DNA and RNA in order that it can continue to know its function. Akasha governs our sense of hearing and our capacity to speak with our own voice. Those in whom this tattva is strongest have great **organizational abilities**. When this tattva loses its vitality we lose the capacity to organize ourselves meaningfully and properly. Conversely we may become obsessed with routine and tidiness.

# Breath and the tattvas

Breath is the means of both accessing and balancing each of these tattvas. Each tattva receives its vitality from the breath. Modern, shallow, hyperventilating breathing hardly feeds and nourishes these tattvas at all. People are left feeling exhausted, dispirited, lost, as each tattva loses contact with the breath. There is a natural withdrawal of the prana towards the end of a person's life – our problem is that we are living that way for forty, fifty and sometimes sixty years, never achieving our full potential.

# Breathing in meditative practices

Enlightenment, from an Eastern perspective, does not happen without the body. It is not something to look forward to after death – it is something we begin to walk towards as embodied beings. Breath is the vital link between inner and outer; up and down; ignorance and enlightenment.

# Breathing Life into Life

There are extremely powerful breathing techniques which not only balance the vitality and allow it to flow freely through the body, but which quiet the mind and prepare it for self awareness and meditation. I suggest that you try the exercises in the Breathing Towards Clarity chapter before you begin these, as a body that is relatively free of tension is a better meditating tool than one in which tension is still firmly fixed.

## Connecting with the physical self

This exercise allows you to become aware of and connect, via the breath, with your inner physical self. It is taken from an ancient Daoist practice which has been modified slightly for use in the West. Sit in a position that is comfortable, in which your back has support and in an environment that feels warm and safe. Then after you have read through the steps of the exercise, close your eyes and try to visualize the whole sequence.

- Become aware of the flow of breath in and out of your body. You are not trying to breathe deeply – you are simply watching your breath with curiosity.
- Become aware of the moment between breaths, the still-point. Enter into the still-point as deeply as you are able – seeking out the moment when the next inhalation begins and the place it begins from.
- Visualize your whole skeleton: the cranial vault that protects your brain, the entire length of the spine, the ribs, the long bones of the arms and hands, the hips and the bones of the legs and feet.
- Breathe in, feeling prana entering your lungs with the breath. As you exhale, this prana is carried throughout the length of the skeleton and wraps around it. During that brief still-point visualize this prana penetrating the skeleton. Repeat this process for three rounds of inhalation, exhalation and still-point.
- Visualize your major internal organs: your heart, your lungs, your stomach, spleen, intestines, kidneys and liver, or choose just one of the major organs – perhaps one that has become weak.

- Breathe in, feeling the prana enter your lungs with the breath. As your body breathes out, feel the prana travelling through the body and wrapping around the organs or single organ. During the brief still-point allow this prana to penetrate the organs you are holding in your visualization. Repeat this process for three more rounds of in-breath, out-breath and still-point.
- Continue in the same way, visualizing prana wrapping itself around first the musculature of your body and then your whole body, from top to toe.

You can allow this exercise to be as complex or as simple as you like. There may be some problem you are experiencing and then you can focus on that area. I always advise that you finish with the 'whole body' breath to keep in mind your wholeness – otherwise it is very easy to become identified with just one part of one's self – usually the part that is not working well.

## Connecting with the pranic self

In this exercise we connect with the points of focus of each tattva and allow the breath to penetrate them, invigorate them and balance them. Again read through the steps and then take a comfortable, supported seat and allow your breath and mind to work in harmonized focus.

- Become aware of the tide of air flowing in and out of your body. Feel its rhythm and be particularly aware of the coolness of the breath as it enters your nose, hits the back of your throat and then enters your lungs. As you exhale become aware that the breath leaving your lungs feels warm as it rises up your throat and leaves through your nose. Be aware of the still-point and the beginning of all breath within it.
- Visualize a radiant hollow tube running from the crown of your head, down your spine, emerging from the base of your spine and continuing down to the perineum. As you breathe in visualize a cool current flowing down this radiant tube, and as you breathe out feel a warm current rising up it. During the still-point visualize the radiance of the tube growing ever brighter. Repeat this three times.
- At the perineum visualize a yellow square that holds the same power as that of the earth: support, stability, cohesion. As you breathe in allow the cool current to connect with that square and flood into it. As you breathe out allow the warm current to flow

from the square, drawing its energy up to the base of the spine. During the still-point feel that the many small currents flowing from this focus of energy are open and receptive to this renewed 'earth' energy.

- This energy of the earth now connects with the base of the spine, the place of focus of water tattva. Visualize the shape of a silvery crescent moon on a dark blue background and be aware that this shape holds all the qualities of water – creativity, will and memory. Breathe in and let the cool current strike open this point of energy and flow into it. As you breathe out allow the warm current to flow up from this crescent moon shape and connect with the place behind the navel. During the still-point feel that the many small currents flowing from this focus of energy are open and receptive to this renewed 'water' energy.

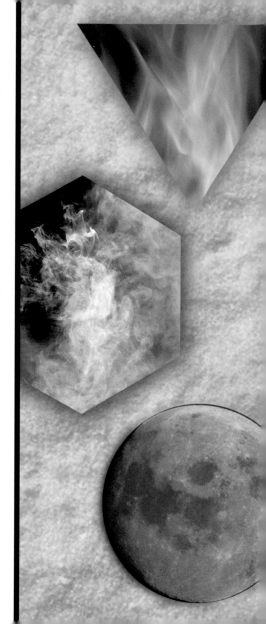

- Now both the earth and water energy have connected to the fire energy behind the navel. Become aware of a fiery triangle with its apex pointed downward – holding the power of transformation and vision. Allow the cool current going down the tube to strike this point of energy, open it, and flow into it as you breathe in. As you breathe out feel the warm current rising and connecting with the point behind the heart. During the still-point feel that the many small currents flowing from this focus of energy are open and receptive to this renewed 'fire' energy.

- The energies of earth, water and fire have now connected with the energy of air. Visualize a smoky hexagonal shape in the space behind the heart carrying the power of air – movement, sensitivity, motivation and lightness of being. As you breathe in allow the cool current to open this point and flow in. As you breathe out let the warm current rise up the tube to the base of the back of the neck. During the still-point feel that the many small currents flowing from this focus are open and receptive to this renewed 'air' energy.

- The energies of earth, water, fire and air have now been connected with the energy of space at the base of the neck. Visualize a white full moon shape at this point holding the energy of organization, order and manifestation. As you breathe in allow the cool current to open this energy point and feel the prana flow in. As you breathe out allow the warm current to rise to the point between your eyebrows. During the still-point feel that the many small currents flowing from this focus are open and receptive to this renewed 'space' energy.

- Now the energies of earth, water, fire, air and space have been drawn to the space between the eyebrows. This particular point is their centre for balance. Breathe into this centre between the eyebrows. Feel it drawing the prana to balance and energize each of the tattvas it is now holding. As you breathe out feel that each tattva is released back down into its focus of energy along the radiant tube. Breathe in and out five times and with each exhalation let one energy return to its base.

Once you have turned your gaze to look at your physical being and your energetic being you can look inward with an enquiring vision. That is the beginning of meditation and enlightenment.

## Breathing beyond breath

This is an exercise used entirely for meditation.

- Become aware of the flow of breath in and out of your body. You are not trying to breathe deeply – you are simply watching your breath with curiosity.
- Become aware of the moment between breaths, the still-point of the body when it balances its needs with the needs of the environment. Enter as deeply as you are able into the still-point – seeking out in it the moment when the next inhalation begins and the place that it begins from.
- Remain in this state of relaxed awareness bringing more and more attention to the still-point. You are actively seeking the beginning of the next breath within this moment of stillness.
- Then there is not another point – there is a gradual flowing towards the question, 'What is breathing me?' That question does not arise without the answer. To find the answer one has to remain with the breath and with the question.

# Ways Forward

If we read none of this book or any other book on breathing our bodies would continue to breathe. However, once we have discovered how deeply personal breathing is – how much it is linked to what we are feeling, thinking and who we are with and in touch with, just breathing can never be the same again. Then it becomes our bridge: our bridge from the conscious to the unconscious; from life to death; from unknowing to knowing. We can use our breathing to help direct us in our own personal unfoldment. To do that we will need the help and guidance of those who themselves have walked some way on the road to piercing the mystery of breath. In this chapter we will look at the possibilities.

# Yoga

Yoga is an excellent place to begin an exploration of breathing. After many years of practising it I am convinced that all the postures of Yoga are there to challenge the way we breathe and forge new breathing habits in our bodies. However, there is no uniformity of teaching in Yoga, so I would strongly suggest you speak to several teachers before you commit to one. Ask them about their particular methodology and how much of its focus is on breathwork. Some of the systems of Yoga have become 'exercise and power' oriented and you will have to do some phonework or legwork to find the right teacher for your needs.

# Hakomi

This is a relatively new and extremely exciting body-oriented psychotherapy. Developed by Ron Kurtz in the mid-1970s it was a culmination of his previous study and experience in psychology, science and philosophy. His great influences were Bioenergetics and some of the ancient philosophies from the East, particularly Daoism and Buddhism. The beauty of Hakomi is that it allows you to explore, in the safest possible environment, the way your body has organized itself around your life experiences, including breathing.

# Meditation

There are now many schools of meditation all over the world. Some Yoga teachers have a particular interest in meditation and may include it as part of their classes. All techniques of meditation will focus on the breath. Quite well advertised is the Buddhist Vipassana meditation. Mindful breathing is very much a core focus of this method.
The Reverend Thich Nhat Hanh, who has a centre in France but whose books are available everywhere, was one of the first teachers to make available the Buddhist techniques of mindful breathing. His works would be a good starting point of your journey if you wish to explore your breathing through meditation.

# Tai Chi and Chi Gong

There has been an explosion of interest in these two systems in the last decade. While neither directly focuses on breathing they use movement with breath to bring our attention to our breathing. They both provide more of a 'bodywork' environment than an exercise one. Tai Chi is actually a martial art but it employs balance and focused attention rather than physical strength. Chi Gong is a system of movement that developed along with acupuncture to correct the imbalance of Qi in the system. Its movements are gentle, opening and explorative rather than goal-seeking and imposing – all ideal for exploring your breathing.

# The Alexander Technique

If you have felt through the exercises in this book that you have a great deal of physical tension that you are unable to dispose of yourself it would be advisable to get help. I have seen the Alexander Technique work absolute wonders for people where tension was so locked into muscle that they were not even aware of its existence. An Alexander teacher will recommend a course of sessions for you to attend. Each session usually lasts about three-quarters of an hour, but its effect can be felt for days. The muscles give up their tension because the teacher, through guided movement, helps you to stop holding onto it.

Tai Chi training using the ►
basic Chi Kung standing
posture.

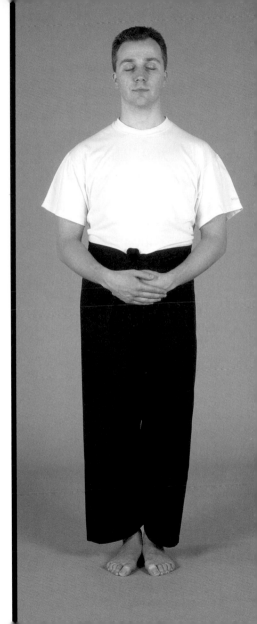

# Resources

## Yoga

**UK**

The Traditional Yoga Association
18 Westminster Way
Lower Earley
Reading
RG6 4BX
Tel: 0118 975 6530

The Yoga for Health
Foundation
Ickwell Bury
Biggleswade
Bedfordshire
SG18 9EF
Tel: 01767 627271

The British Wheel of Yoga
1 Hamilton Place
Boston Road
Sleaford
Lincolnshire
NG34 7ES
Tel: 01529 303233

The Iyengar Yoga Institute
223a Randolph Avenue
London
W9 1NL
Tel: 020 7624 3080

**USA**

The Yoga Journal Magazine
2054 University Avenue
Berkeley, CA 94704
Tel: 510 841 9200

Yoga International's Guide to
Yoga Teachers and Classes
RR1, Box 407
Honesdale, PA 18431
Tel: 800 821-YOGA

## Breathwork Teachers

**USA**
Gay Hendricks
The Hendricks Institute
409 East Bijou Street
Colorado Springs
CO 80903
Tel: 800 688 0772

Somatic Resources
PO Box 2067
Berkeley
CA 94702
Tel: 510 540 7600

The Middendorf Breath Institute
198 Mississippi
San Francisco
CA 94107
Tel: 415 255 2174

## Body Centred Psychotherapy

**UK**
Hakomi UK
18 South Street
Lewes
East Sussex
Tel: 01273 706511

**USA**
The Hakomi Institute
PO Box 1873
Boulder
CO 80306
Tel: 303 499 6699

## The Alexander Technique

Society of Teachers of the
Alexander Technique
10 London House
266 Fulham Road
London
SW10 9E1
Tel: 020 7351 0828

## The Buteyko Method

The Hale Clinic
7 Park Cresent
London
W1N 3HE
Tel: 020 763 0156

## Meditation

London Buddhist Centre
51 Roman Road
London
E2 0HU
Tel: 020 8981 1225

The Reverend Thich Nhat Hanh
Village des Pruniers
Meyrace
47120 Loubes-Bernac
France
Tel: 33 (0)16 53 96 75 40